LEADERS LIKE

WENDELL SCOTT

BY J. P. MILLER

ILLUSTRATED BY
AMANDA QUARTEY

Rourke

BEFORE AND DURING READING ACTIVITIES

Before Reading: *Building Background Knowledge and Vocabulary*

Building background knowledge can help children process new information and build upon what they already know. Before reading a book, it is important to tap into what children already know about the topic. This will help them develop their vocabulary and increase their reading comprehension.

Questions and Activities to Build Background Knowledge:

1. Look at the front cover of the book and read the title. What do you think this book will be about?
2. What do you already know about this topic?
3. Take a book walk and skim the pages. Look at the table of contents, photographs, captions, and bold words. Did these text features give you any information or predictions about what you will read in this book?

Vocabulary: *Vocabulary Is Key to Reading Comprehension*

Use the following directions to prompt a conversation about each word.

- Read the vocabulary words.
- What comes to mind when you see each word?
- What do you think each word means?

Vocabulary Words:
- career
- compete
- division
- inducted
- promoters
- replica
- segregated
- sponsors

During Reading: *Reading for Meaning and Understanding*

To achieve deep comprehension of a book, children are encouraged to use close reading strategies. During reading, it is important to have children stop and make connections. These connections result in deeper analysis and understanding of a book.

 Close Reading a Text

During reading, have children stop and talk about the following:

- Any confusing parts
- Any unknown words
- Text to text, text to self, text to world connections
- The main idea in each chapter or heading

Encourage children to use context clues to determine the meaning of any unknown words. These strategies will help children learn to analyze the text more thoroughly as they read.

When you are finished reading this book, turn to the next-to-last page for **Text-Dependent Questions** and an **Extension Activity**.

TABLE OF CONTENTS

COURAGE
TO BE
GREAT

Have you ever wanted to try something daring? Have you ever wanted to be the first to do something? Wendell Scott liked to drive fast. He wanted to be a champion stock car racer. He was the first Black person to win a major National Association of Stock Car Auto Racing (NASCAR) race.

"Drivers, start your engines!" said the NASCAR grand marshal. Wendell stomped on the gas pedal. He wanted to win the Jacksonville 200, a championship NASCAR race. Off he went, like he did on the streets back home in Danville, Virginia. That night in Jacksonville, Florida, Wendell took car number 34 across the finish line first.

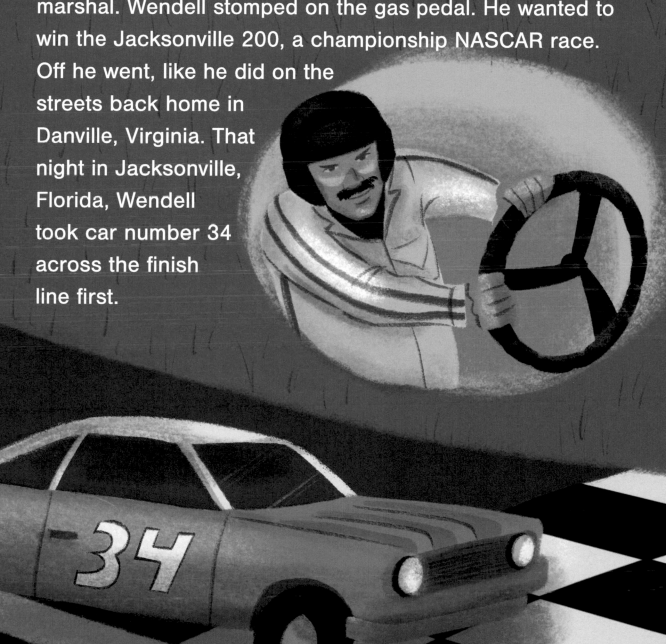

To Wendell's surprise, there was no checkered flag that said he won the race. The title was awarded to a white driver. That angered Wendell. He argued his victory for hours. After the crowd left, NASCAR finally declared him the winner. He got the prize money, but he never received the trophy.

TOP SERIES

The Jacksonville 200 was the third race of the 1964 NASCAR Grand National Series. The series had a total of 62 races.

HARD TIMES

    As a young boy, Wendell watched his father repair cars. He studied each tool and how it was used. Before long, he was fixing bicycles for children in his neighborhood. After that, he repaired cars.

    Wendell had a knack for speed. He drove his car too fast all the time. In a year's time, he got at least ten speeding tickets. Instead of getting in trouble, the police gave his name to stock car racing promoters. The **promoters** wanted to hire Black drivers and allow them to race too. If Wendell could outrun the police, surely he could win races.

As Wendell grew up, he continued to race. He started winning more. He hitched his race car to his truck and drove to South Carolina. His two sons went along to help. He was headed to the Spartanburg Fairgrounds for his first Grand National series race. He had qualified for NASCAR's major **division**.

FIX IT!

Pit crews fix race cars in the middle of a race. Wendell could not afford one, so he created his own and called it Scott Racing. His two sons and other relatives worked with him. Wendell would sometimes get out of his car during a race, fix his car, and hop back in to finish the race.

Hard times were ahead, though. The American South was very **segregated**. Many people did not like Wendell because he was Black. Racing fans booed him. White drivers tried to run into his car and make him crash. Race officials refused to pay him. A hate group called the Ku Klux Klan tried to scare Wendell away from racing. They could not stop him.

MORE WITH LESS

During his **career**, Wendell had always used old car parts. It was the only way he could afford to keep his car running. He was envious of the white drivers who had lots of money and many **sponsors**.

They got **new cars...**

...new engines...

...and the best pit crews.

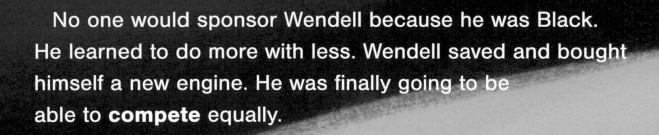

No one would sponsor Wendell because he was Black. He learned to do more with less. Wendell saved and bought himself a new engine. He was finally going to be able to **compete** equally.

The cool Alabama night was perfect for racing. The Winston 500 race was Wendell's first one with the new engine. He was excited for his new beginning. When the grand marshal told the drivers to start their engines, he gladly flipped his car's switch. He was ready to win.

E

START

The heat from his engine sliced through the cold air. Wendell drove the track faster than ever before. During his first lap, he settled in. By his fifth lap, he was doing well and feeling proud. But in his tenth lap, something went wrong.

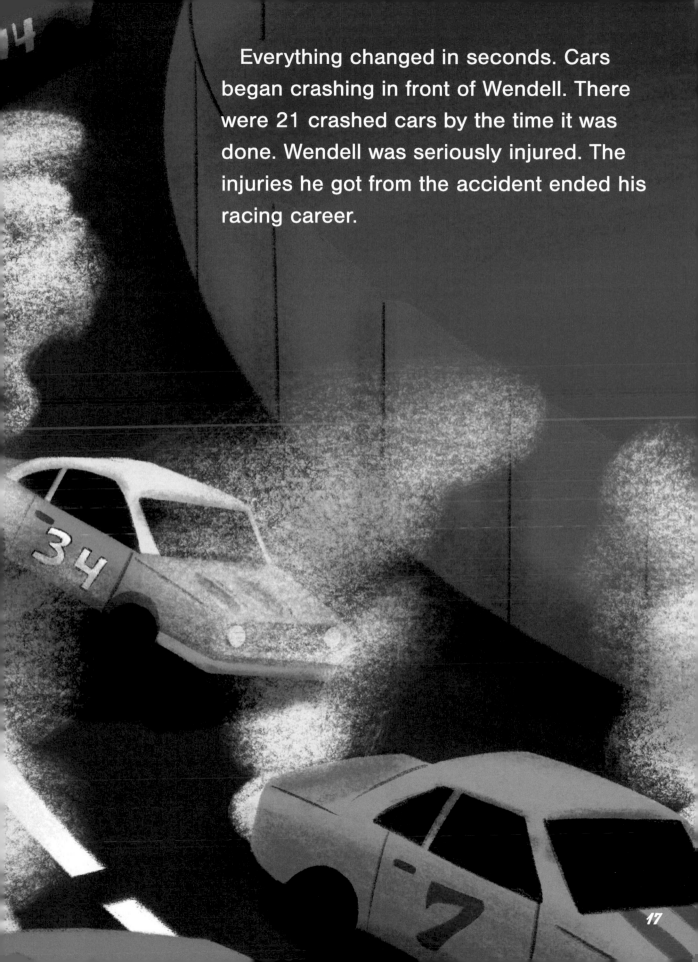

Everything changed in seconds. Cars began crashing in front of Wendell. There were 21 crashed cars by the time it was done. Wendell was seriously injured. The injuries he got from the accident ended his racing career.

After the crash, Wendell retired. He opened an auto repair shop in his community. Wendell was **inducted** into the Black Athletes Hall of Fame. A movie based on his life was made called *Greased Lightning*.

GREASED
LIGHTNING

GREASED
LIGHTNING

A TRUE WINNER

Wendell Scott was very good at racing. Wendell had 495 starts, 1 victory, 20 top 5s, 147 top 10s, and 1 pole position in his races combined.

Wendell Scott died on December 23rd, 1990. He was inducted into the NASCAR Hall of Fame in 2015. In 2010, his family received a **replica** of the Jacksonville 200 trophy that Wendell never received.

Wendell Scott never thought of himself as a leader. He just wanted to be great at what he did. He showed many people how to be courageous and win in the end.

"When it's too tough for everybody else, it's just right for me.
—Wendell Scott"

TIME LINE

1921 Wendell Oliver Scott is born on August 29th in Danville, Virginia.

1943 He marries Mary Coles. They eventually have seven children.

1947 Wendell has his first race at the Danville Fairgrounds NASCAR Dixie Circuit. He places 3rd and wins $50.

1961 He crosses over into NASCAR's major division. His debut race is the Grand National Series race at the Spartanburg Fairgrounds in South Carolina.

1963 Wendell wins his first Grand National Series race at Speedway Park in Jacksonville, Florida, on December 1st. He becomes the first Black driver to win a race at NASCAR's highest level. A white man is awarded the victory instead of Wendell.

1973 Wendell has a career-ending crash at the Talladega Speedway in Alabama. He retires from racing and opens an auto repair shop.

1977 The hit movie *Greased Lightning*, starring Richard Pryor, is released. It is based loosely on the life of Wendell Scott.

1977 Wendell is inducted in the Black Athletes Hall of Fame.

1990 Wendell Scott dies on December 23rd. He is buried in his hometown of Danville, Virginia.

2010 The Scott family is presented with a replica of Wendell's long-lost winner's trophy from the 1963 race in Jacksonville.

2015 Wendell is inducted into the NASCAR Hall of Fame.

2017 Pixar releases the animated movie *Cars 3*, which includes a character based on Wendell. The character is a car with the number 34, the same number as Wendell Scott's car.

GLOSSARY

career (kuh-REER): the work or the series of jobs that a person has

compete (kuhm-PEET): to try hard to outdo others at a task, race, or contest

division (di-VIZH-uhn): a part of an organization that does some things independently

inducted (in-DUK-ted): put into a place of honor, such as a hall of fame

promoters (pruh-MOTE-urz): people who help with the growth or development of something

replica (REP-li-kuh): an exact copy of something

segregated (SEG-ri-gay-ted): separated from the main group on the basis of things such as race or gender

sponsors (SPAHN-surs): a person or group that pays some or all of the costs involved in holding a sporting or artistic event in return for advertising

INDEX

TEXT-DEPENDENT QUESTIONS

1. How did Wendell Scott get his start in auto racing?
2. Why was it so important when Wendell Scott won the Jacksonville 200?
3. Why was Wendell Scott unable to get a sponsor?
4. What movie was based on Wendell Scott's life?
5. In what ways was Wendell Scott a leader?

EXTENSION ACTIVITY

Try something new! Think of four adventurous activities you have never done before, such as hiking, visiting a new place, or learning a new skill. Research to learn more about the activities and where you can do them. Next, choose any month of the year and do one of the adventurous activities with your family.

ABOUT THE AUTHOR

J. P. Miller Growing up, J. P. Miller loved reading stories that she could become immersed in. As a writer, she enjoys doing the same for her readers. Through the gift of storytelling, she is able to bring little- and well-known people and events in African American history to life for young readers. She hopes that her stories will augment the classroom experience and inspire her readers. J. P. lives in metro Atlanta and is the author of the *Careers in the US Military* and *Black Stories Matter* series.

ABOUT THE ILLUSTRATOR

Amanda Quartey Amanda lives in the UK and was born and bred in London. She has always loved to draw and has been doing so ever since she can remember. At the age of 14, she moved to Ghana and studied art in school. She later returned to the UK to study graphic design. Her artistic path deviated slightly when she studied Classics at her university. Over the years, in a bid to return to her artistic roots, Amanda has built a professional illustration portfolio and is now loving every bit of her illustration career.

www.rourkebooks.com

Quote source: Scott, Frank. "African-American NASCAR Driver Raced 'Like a Great Artist'," *StoryCorps,* NPR, January 30, 2015.

Edited by: Tracie Santos
Illustrations by: Amanda Quartey
Cover and interior layout by: J. J. Giddings

Library of Congress PCN Data

Wendell Scott / J. P. Miller
(Leaders Like Us)
ISBN 978-1-73164-928-7 (hard cover)
ISBN 978-1-73164-876-1 (soft cover)
ISBN 978-1-73164-980-5 (e-Book)
ISBN 978-1-73165-032-0 (ePub)
Library of Congress Control Number: 2021935460

Rourke Educational Media
Printed in the United States of America
05-1342411937